Divine Treasure

Divine Treasure

THE PROVERBS 31 FINANCIAL PLAN TO GIVE YOU HOPE FOR YOUR FUTURE

§

Carolyn Castleberry Hux

A Faith and Women Ministries, Inc. Publication
ISBN (hardcover): 0999611100
ISBN (eBook): 9780999611104
Library of Congress Control Number: 2017919013
Faith and Women Ministries, Inc., Virginia Beach, VA

Divine Treasure: The Proverbs 31 Financial Plan to Give You Hope for Your Future. Lesson 1–The Least You Need to Know About Money © 2018 by Carolyn Castleberry Hux

Unless otherwise indicated, Scripture quotations are from: New American Standard Bible ® (NASB) © 1960, 1977, 1995 by the Lockman Foundation. Used by permission.
Other Scripture quotations are from: *The Holy Bible,* New International Version (NIV) © 1973, 1984 by International Bible Society, used by permission of Zondervan Publishing House.
The Message © 1993, 1994, 1995, 1996, 2000, 2001, 2002 Used by permission of NavPress Publishing Group.
Contemporary English Version (CEV) © 1995 by American Bible Society.
The New Life Version (NLV) © Christian Literature International, 1969.
Holy Bible, New Living Translation (NLV) © 1996. Used by permission of Tyndale House Publishers, Inc.
All rights reserved.

For information:
Faith and Women Ministries, Inc.
PO Box 6871
Virginia Beach, VA 23456
www.faithandwomen.org

Lesson 1
The Least You Need to Know About Money
Includes study questions and worksheets

Contents

Introduction

§

WHEN I FIRST BEGAN PUBLISHING financial and time management books in 2006, life looked and felt much different. Our country had yet to experience the greatest time of economic trial since the Great Depression. While many of the economic pundits on television talk of an economic recovery on Wall Street, millions of Americans on Main Street are still scratching their heads saying, "What about me and my family?" This was true for my own family. I had yet to go through one of the most excruciating times of my life and the end of a twenty-four-year marriage.

Fortunately for me, for you, and for our country there is hope. Hope that never failed even during our darkest, poorest, loneliest hours. Hope has a name: Jesus. He never left you. You may (or may not) feel this is a time of renewal and new hope for our country, depending on which political side you identify with. To this I say it matters, and it doesn't. Yes, there are practical economic issues to consider for your family, but there are spiritual principles of money that never change.

If you grew up in a faith community, you may have heard this head-scratching passage from the book of James on trials and temptations, "Consider it pure joy, my brothers and sisters, whenever you face trials of many kinds, because you know that the testing of your faith produces perseverance. Let perseverance finish its work so that you may be mature and complete, not lacking anything" (James 1:2–4, NIV).

Pure joy? You have to be kidding, you say. I know I've thought it. Facing trials and the testing of our faith is anything but fun, especially when it hits our pocketbooks. *The Message*'s paraphrased version of this passage, however, adds additional perspective to the purpose of trials in our lives when our faith is under pressure:

Consider it a sheer gift, friends, when tests and challenges come at you from all sides. You know that under pressure, your faith-life is forced into the open and shows its true colors. So don't try to get out of anything prematurely. Let it do its work so you become mature and well developed, not deficient in any way. (James 1:2–4 MSG)

God first needs to work *on us* before He can work *through us*, and times of trial don't last forever when you're walking this journey with the Lord of all resources.

For now let's begin with a firm foundation grounded in the knowledge that God has been with you all along in your valleys of life. Money—or the lack thereof—is one of the tools the Lord uses to build our faith and character if we let him. Like it or not, money matters. It's the stuff we fight about at home but rarely discuss in public. We have no problem talking about our families, our hopes and dreams, or our fears in our faith communities, but mention money and people freeze. It's so much easier not to deal with it.

Here's the reality: God wants us to deal with it in his way. There are more than two thousand verses in the Bible that reference money or possessions. Clearly our Lord knew this would be a challenge for us, and yet this is an issue we are hesitant to fully address in our church communities, especially among women. But here's the wake-up call, according to the National Center for Women and Retirement Research (NCWRR): among women thirty-five to fifty-five years old, between one-third and two-thirds will be impoverished by age seventy. And women live an average of seven years longer than men. That means many of us will have no choice but to personally handle our own finances at some point. In our country we are seeing this scene play out as the baby boomer population ages.

I understand your tendency to feel overwhelmed by finances, but my hope is *The Proverbs 31 Financial Plan* will give you new confidence and hope for your future. My intention is to build your faith in the Lord who provides for you and to build your confidence to begin a new financial journey. This is a divine treasure for your peace of mind, no matter what your bank statement looks like this month.

Nearly a decade ago, I began this writing journey with women in mind. Since that time, working as a financial advisor and learning from two of the top male entrepreneurs in this country, Pat Robertson of CBN and John Hewitt of Jackson Hewitt and Liberty Tax Service, I have come to realize that this financial plan, modeled by a woman whom God placed in the Bible thousands of years ago, is a plan that can help both women and men succeed today. Your path will never be perfect. I've never met anyone in life who hasn't struggled with financial issues to some extent. I've faced down debt, divorce, and financial fear and come to the realization that my true security is in God alone.

This is why *Divine Treasure* is about much more than just managing dollars. It's about finding your purpose in the only one who truly knows what you were created to do. That's because God is the one who did the creating. He loved every moment of it and has never stopped loving you. "For we are His workmanship, created in Christ Jesus for good works, which God prepared beforehand so that we would walk in them." (Ephesians 2:10)

In working out your purpose, He never intended you to navigate your life as a slave to money. Through God money is subservient to you. So let's walk down this path together, taking our time and learning to carefully consider our ever-growing number of financial options. The journey in *Divine Treasure* begins with understanding both the spiritual and practical laws of money.

On a personal note, at the spry age of fifty-three, God brought me the man of my dreams: Ernie Hux. We were married on November 24, 2017, which was also my parents sixty-sixth anniversary and his parents' fifty-seventh anniversary. Miracles still do happen.

And there is still a happy ending for you.

PART I

Five Spiritual Reality Checks
for Your Checkbook

CHAPTER 1

Embrace Your True Financial Partner

HERE'S A HEADLINE YOU WON'T see on any financial planning brochure: *There is No Such Thing As Financial Security*. Working as a financial advisor, I could never shake this scripture I learned as a child in church, "Do not store up for yourselves treasures on earth, where moth and rust destroy, and where thieves break in and steal. But store up for yourselves treasures in heaven, where moth and rust do not destroy, and where thieves do not break in and steal." (Matthew 6:19–20) In our lifetime we may want to replace the words moth and rust with recession and joblessness.

However, while there may not be financial security on this earth, there is a different kind of security. It will never depend on the numbers—or lack thereof—on your bank statement. True security, the kind that brings deep peace and joy, only comes from God. Your plan for freedom and purpose won't work until and unless you commit your work to Him. "Unless the Lord builds the house, they labor in vain who build it." (Psalm 127:1)

I wasted many years asking God to get on board with *my* plans, instead of working in the flow of His will. I had to learn the following Old Testament lesson the hard way: "It is the Lord your God you must follow, and Him you must revere. Keep His commands and obey Him; serve Him and hold fast to Him." (Deuteronomy 13:4) This is an age-old lesson that still stands today and is the beginning of your true security. Plus he hasn't left you alone to work out your best financial equation; He has promised to be your true financial advisor. But here's the problem: unless we're spending time with Him, how can we hear His voice? A Psalm of David reads, "Give ear to my words, O Lord, consider my sighing. Listen to my cry for help, my King and my God, for to you I pray. In the morning, O Lord, you hear my voice; in the morning I lay my requests before you and wait in expectation." (Psalm 5:1–3)

One day when I was having a time of prayer and reading, I began daydreaming and eventually fell asleep. So much for showing respect to the person I was meeting with, right? As I awakened with a start, I realized I would never behave this way if I were meeting with my boss at my work place. But that's how I was treating my time with my Lord and top advisor. Yes, God is merciful and understanding even when we fall asleep. Remember Peter and the disciples who couldn't keep watch with Jesus for an hour? But if we're seeking direction and guidance from the true chief executive officer, perhaps we should approach him as such.

Many people like to call this a "devotional time" or a "quiet time." I call this my meeting with my CEO. Knowing that "I can do all things through Christ who strengthens me" (Philippians 4:13) gives me extra strength for the day. On the other hand, I know that I can do nothing without him, or at least nothing very well. Many times in my life, God has astonishingly used this meeting with Him as a precise guide to get me through the challenges of the day. Without this time with God, I invariably flounder. If I take just a few moments to quiet my mind and my heart, my entire day goes by more smoothly, and I feel more capable in managing challenges.

In Jeremiah 29:11, the Lord promises His people that He has a plan for us to give us a future and a hope. What He says next is this:

> "Then you will call upon Me and come and pray to Me, and I will listen to you. You will seek Me and find Me when you search for Me with all your heart. I will be found by you…" (Jeremiah 29:12)

God will be found by you if you seek Him and search for Him with all your heart.

Have you ever been discouraged when it seems God isn't listening or maybe He's forgotten about you? I have. And though He hasn't forgotten us or stopped listening, we have to persevere. Keep searching and keep meeting with your chief executive officer, and His plans will become clear. Knowing God's vision in this way makes all the difference in whether we succeed in getting a handle on our financial life. And that, my friend, takes time—plus patient, believing prayer:

> If any of you lacks wisdom, let him ask of God, who gives to all generously and without reproach, and it will be given to him. But he must ask in faith without any doubting, for the one who doubts is like the surf of the sea, driven and tossed by the wind. (James 1:5–6)

We've all been confused. I know what it's like to feel full of doubt and tossed by the wind. As a young woman, I certainly understood and lived that way. But as I've grown older, and hopefully a bit wiser, I know without any doubt that God answers us when we call to Him. It may not be instantaneous, and it may not be the answer you're looking for, but He gives us the right answer that's best for us and our situations. When we ask for wisdom, God always, always delivers. That's a promise. And after you've asked for help, expect answers. Expect action on the Lord's part and learn to wait for Him. Don't ever forget the Lord and His grace to you. And as you faithfully remember, you will know His blessing more than ever:

> If you fully obey the Lord your God and carefully follow all his commands I give you today, the Lord your God will set you high above all the nations on earth. All these blessings will come upon you and accompany you if you obey the Lord your God:

You will be blessed in the city and blessed in the country.

The fruit of your womb will be blessed, and the crops of your land and the young of your livestock-the calves of your herds and the lambs of your flocks.

Your basket and your kneading trough will be blessed.

You will be blessed when you come in and blessed when you go out.

The Lord will grant that the enemies who rise up against you will be defeated before you. They will come at you from one direction but flee from you in seven.

The Lord will send a blessing on your barns and on everything you put your hand to. The Lord your God will bless you in the land he is giving you.

The Lord will establish you as his holy people, as he promised you on oath, if you keep the commands of the Lord your God and walk in his ways. Then all the peoples on earth will see that you are called by the name of the Lord, and they will fear you. The Lord will grant you abundant prosperity—in the fruit of your womb, the young of your livestock and the crops of your ground— in the land he swore to your forefathers to give you.

The Lord will open the heavens, the storehouse of his bounty, to send rain on your land in season and to bless all the work of your hands. You will lend to many nations but will borrow from none. The Lord will make you the head, not the tail. If you pay attention to the commands of the Lord your God that I give you this day and carefully follow them, you will always be at the top, never at the bottom. Do not turn aside from any of the commands I give you today, to the right or to the left, following other gods and serving them. (Deuteronomy 28:1–14, NIV)

Questions to Go Deeper

1. Be honest. One of the hardest things to do is to truly commit our financial future to God. In *How to Manage Your Money*, Larry Burkett writes that one way to apply God's principles to our money matters is through "Financial Breathing"—exhaling bad habits and inhaling good principles.[1] He says that first of all, we must daily acknowledge God's ownership of our assets:

---

1 Larry Burkett, *How to Manage Your Money* (Chicago: Moody Press, 1982), 51–59.

Trust in the LORD with all your heart and do not lean on your own understanding. In all your ways acknowledge Him, and He will make your paths straight. (Proverbs 3:5–6)

Take an inventory of your assets—the possessions that matters most to you—what do you need to give up to the Lord? What are you holding on to tightly?

_____

_____

_____

_____

_____

_____

2. Next, according to Burkett, we must accept God's answers and direction and breathe in His goodness and wisdom. Just as parents know what's best for their children, God knows and does what's best for us:

If you then, being evil, know how to give good gifts to your children, how much more will your Father who is in heaven give what is good to those who ask Him! (Matthew 7:11)

Think about how much you care for your children, family members, and friends. How much more does your Father care for you? When have you felt His love for you in the past?

_____

_____

_____

_____

_____

_____

3. How has God provided for your needs during your most challenging time?

_____

_____

_____

_____

_____

_____

_____

4. How can you commit your work to the Lord today? What do you strongly feel are His plans for your life?

_____

_____

_____

_____

_____

_____

_____

_____

5. What frightens you most about this process? Remember, you are in strong and capable hands.

_____

_____

_____

_____

_____

_____

Here's a prayer we could all use.

Search me, O God, and know my heart; try me and know my anxious thoughts; and see if there be any hurtful way in me, and lead me in the everlasting way. (Psalm 139:23–24, NIV)

Another version puts it this way:

God, see what is in my heart. Know what is there. Put me to the test. Know what I'm thinking. See if there is anything in my life you don't like. Help me live in the way that is always right. (NIRV)

PEACE AND HOPE FOR FINANCIAL ANXIETY

When you put God at the top of your financial plan, a side benefit is a cure for anxiety:

For this reason I say to you, do not be worried about your life, as to what you will eat or what you will drink; nor for your body, as to what you will put on. Is not life more than food, and the body more than clothing? Look at the birds of the air, that they do not sow, nor reap nor gather into barns, and yet your heavenly Father feeds them. Are you not worth much more than they? And who of you by being worried can add a single hour to his life? And why are you worried about clothing? Observe how the lilies of the field grow; they do not toil nor do they spin, yet I say to you that not even Solomon in all his glory clothed himself like one of these. But if God so clothes the grass of the field, which is alive today and tomorrow is thrown into the furnace, will He not much more clothe you? You of little faith! Do not worry then, saying, "What will we eat?" or "What will we drink?" or "What will we wear for clothing?" For the Gentiles eagerly seek all these things; for your heavenly Father knows that you need all these things. But seek first His kingdom and His righteousness, and all these things will be added to you.

So do not worry about tomorrow; for tomorrow will care for itself. Each day has enough trouble of its own. (Matthew 6:25–34, NASB)

Commit your work to the one who knows you and loves you more than anyone else.

NOTES:

_____

_____

_____

_____

_____

_____

_____

_____

_____

_____

_____

_____

_____

_____

_____

_____

CHAPTER 2

The Bible's Premier Female Investor

An excellent wife, who can find?
For her worth is far above jewels.
The heart of her husband trusts in her,
And he will have no lack of gain.
She does him good and not evil
All the days of her life.
She looks for wool and flax
And works with her hands in delight.
She is like merchant ships;
She brings her food from afar.
She rises also while it is still night
And gives food to her household
And portions to her maidens.
She considers a field and buys it;
From her earnings she plants a vineyard.
She girds herself with strength
And makes her arms strong.
She senses that her gain is good;
Her lamp does not go out at night.
She stretches out her hands to the distaff,
And her hands grasp the spindle.
She extends her hand to the poor,
And she stretches out her hands to the needy.
She is not afraid of the snow for her household,
For all her household are clothed with scarlet.
She makes coverings for herself;
Her clothing is fine linen and purple.
Her husband is known in the gates,

When he sits among the elders of the land.
She makes linen garments and sells them,
And supplies belts to the tradesmen.
Strength and dignity are her clothing,
And she smiles at the future.
She opens her mouth in wisdom,
And the teaching of kindness is on her tongue.
She looks well to the ways of her household,
And does not eat the bread of idleness.
Her children rise up and bless her;
Her husband also, and he praises her, saying:
"Many daughters have done nobly,
But you excel them all."
Charm is deceitful and beauty is vain,
But a woman who fears the Lord, she shall be praised.
Give her the product of her hands,
And let her works praise her in the gates. (Proverbs 31:10–31)

WITH GOD AS YOUR TOP financial advisor, there are a number of people who God can bring into your life to show you how to be victorious in your finances. You can learn from many of them and in another lesson of *Divine Treasure*, in which we'll look at the strategies and questions you need to build a wise and trustworthy team, based on results.

For now let me introduce you to someone we all can learn from. This is a person who stands out as a person of character, a hard worker, and an astute financial model. And I love the fact that she's a woman. I hope you also discover that she's someone much like you, though she lived in an age that was less kind to women than ours is, one that didn't afford them all the opportunities we have now. She juggled relationships and career and took it one step further; she became an investor, just as you can. An investor in God. An investor in her family. And an investor in business—in something that would provide financially for her family long into the future.

In contrast to the nagging, adulterous, mean-spirited female images in much of Proverbs, the woman in chapter 31 is God fearing, strong, wise, and immensely capable. Did this woman truly exist, with all these positive attributes? Or was she simply a figment of the author's wishful imagination in creating a model for the rest of us to follow?

I don't think it matters. If we believe all scripture is inspired by God and beneficial for our training in righteousness, then we would be wise to accept that there are many lessons to be learned from the woman in Proverbs 31. Lessons of family, virtue, and honor.

Let's take a closer look at this remarkable woman from Proverbs 31. Love her or hate her, you have to admit she's a breath of fresh air in a long lineup of other female mug shots depicted in

Proverbs. As Ann Spangler and Jean Syswerda observe in *Women of the Bible*, Proverbs overflows with less-than-glowing descriptions of women. There are wayward wives, prostitutes, and women with smoother-than-oil lips. We find strange women, loud women, defiant women, and wives who are like a continual drip on a rainy day or decay in their husbands' bones. There are women whose feet never stay home, brazen-faced women, and even a woman so repulsive she's likened to a gold ring in a pig's snout!

However, the book of Proverbs opens and closes with positive portrayals of women: first, a woman personified as wisdom (in Proverbs 3–4 and 8–9), and then finally, in Proverbs 31, an "excellent wife" who seemingly can do no wrong.

- She put God at the top of her priority list. "Charm is deceitful and beauty is vain, but a woman who fears the Lord, she shall be praised" (verse 30).
- She made family her next priority: "She is not afraid of the snow for her household, for all her household are clothed with scarlet" (verse 21). "Her children rise up and bless her" (verse 28).
- She had a positive outlook and as a result, "she smiles at the future" (verse 25).
- She put her creative talents to work. "She looks for wood and flax, and works with her hands in delight." (verse 13) "She makes linen garments and sells them, and supplies belts to the tradesmen" (verse 24).
- She was a careful investor. "She considers a field and buys it; from her earnings she plants a vineyard" (verse 16).
- She was a hard worker. "She stretches out her hands to the distaff [a weaving device], and her hands grasp the spindle" (verse 19).
- She was generous. "She extends her hand to the poor; and she stretches out her hands to the needy" (verses 19–20).
- She was tough. "Strength and dignity are her clothing" (verse 25); she "girds herself with strength, and makes her arms strong" (verse 17). And she was tireless: She "rises while it is still night" (verse 15) and "her lamp doesn't go out at night" (verse 18).
- She reaped positive rewards. "The heart of her husband trusts in her, and he will have no lack of gain" (verse 11). "Give her the product of her hands, and let her works praise her in the gates" (verse 31).

Do you hate her yet? Many women do because her example has been thrown into the faces of ordinary women who feel they can't possibly live up to her standards. But let's take another look at this remarkable woman from Proverbs 31 and discover what she can teach us about ourselves and how to use our money.

Clearly this mom was very much involved in her family's financial life. And remember this resourceful lady didn't have a laptop or any other high-tech tools to work with. She worked with what she had at the time. Notice that the passage doesn't say her husband did all the work and gave her a shopping allowance. With her own talents and effort, she created both immediate and future wealth and provision for her family.

The Proverbs 31 Financial Plan can be summed up in three simple words: **create, consider, and invest**. This amazing woman created products, she considered her field of investment, and then she actually purchased it.

The Proverbs 31 money model begins with the ability to *create*, by working with your hands and your mind. Traditionally Hebrew women spent huge amounts of time spinning and weaving material for clothing, rugs, and other household needs. These were resourceful women who took wool from sheep or fibers from plants like cotton and flax and spun them into thread. Some linen was so finely woven that it formed silky, rich material. Waterproof tents and coats were made with heavy cloth from goat or camel hair.

These women were hard working and amazingly creative. Proverbs 31 adds another element: She was energetic, working in delight. When she wasn't sewing clothes, making belts, or negotiating with tradesmen, she was looking for wool and flax and bringing her wares from all over the city to be sold at market. She made clothes for herself and her family using the finest material she could find.

The Proverbs 31 woman went on to consider a field and buys it: "From her earnings she plants a vineyard." Nearly every English translation uses the word *consider* here. Dictionaries tell us that *to consider* means to fix your mind on something in order to understand to it. It means to reflect on something with care, to ponder it, to study it, to meditate on it. It means to attentively and carefully view or observe or examine something, to think about it seriously, maturely, or carefully.

Finally she had the courage to invest. Proverbs 31 took action. It had to be overwhelming taking care of her family, creating products for the tradesmen, and all while planting a vineyard. However, this is an investment that would provide multiple streams of income and provide for her family for generations to come. As a woman in that society, men would quickly laugh at her should she make a mistake. And yet we read that she "smiles at the future."

You can do the same thing in your life in God's way. Create, consider, and invest for your future.

QUESTIONS TO GO DEEPER

1. Focus on Proverbs 31:12, 21, 27, 28, and 30. What do these verses tell you about this woman's priorities?

_____

_____

_____

_____

_____

_____

2. Our actions tend to speak infinitely louder than any of our words. Prayerfully consider what your current schedule, lifestyle, habits, and actions reveal about your priorities. In what ways do you sense God may want you to change?

_____

_____

_____

_____

_____

_____

_____

3. Proverbs 31:25 tells us that Proven "smiles at the future." Look through this passage about her life (verses 10–31). What reasons does this woman have for a secure and positive outlook?

_____

_____

_____

_____

_____

_____

4. What is your current attitude about money and your family's finances? Envision five, ten, or twenty years from now. What would it take for you to "smile at the future"?

_____

_____

_____

_____

_____

_____

_____

5. Look at each of the following verses in Proverbs 31 separately. What do they reveal about this woman's personality or character?

verse 11—

_____

_____

_____

_____

_____

_____

verses 14–15—

_____

_____

_____

_____

_____

_____

_____

verse 17—

_____

_____

_____

_____

_____

_____

verse 20—

_____

_____

_____

_____

_____

_____

verses 25–26—

_____

_____

_____

_____

_____

_____

6. How do you already see those character traits at work in your life?

_____

_____

_____

_____

_____

_____

_____

7. Reread the entire passage one more time. In what ways is the Proverbs 31 woman providing for her family? How is she achieving these goals?

_____

_____

_____

_____

_____

_____

8. Read Proverbs 31:16. What is happening in this verse? How does this affect her family's present situation and their future?

_____

_____

_____

_____

_____

_____

_____

9. What does the Bible say about this woman's husband's role in creating income and wealth for her family? How does this apply to you personally today?

_____

_____

_____

_____

_____

_____

10. Finally, if we're honest, we all desire some sort of reward for the work we do, for the time we spend and invest in something. Take a look at Proverbs 31, verses 10–11, 13, 18, 21, 22, 23, 25, and 28–31. How would you describe each of the rewards she received for her efforts and hard work? List each reward or benefit of her behavior.

_____

_____

_____

_____

_____

_____

_____

11. From this list, what rewards would personally mean the most to you?

_____

_____

_____

_____

_____

_____

Charm is deceitful and beauty is vain, but a woman who fears the Lord, she shall be praised. Give her the product of her hands, and let her works praise her in the gates.

(PROVERBS 31:30–31)

NOTES:

CHAPTER 3

Our Responsibility to Invest God-Given Talents

§

THE PROVERBS 31 FINANCIAL MODEL is consistent with New Testament lessons on money. The Gospel of Matthew records a story Jesus told to illustrate our financial responsibilities. It begins with a man who went on a trip and left his servants money (also referred to as "talents") to invest—each according to his ability. He gave one servant five talents, another two talents, and the last servant one talent. When the boss went away, the servants went to work—or at least two of them did—taking risks, doubling their money, and receiving a reward and praise from him when he got back home. But the last servant was afraid and buried his talent in the sand. Let's read about this last guy as the moment came to face his boss:

> He said, "Sir, I know that you are a hard man. You gather grain where you have not planted. You take up where you have not spread out. I was afraid and I hid your money in the ground. See! Here is your money." His owner said to him, "You bad and lazy servant. You knew that I gather grain where I have not planted. You knew that I take up where I have not spread out. You should have taken my money to the bank. When I came back, I could have had my own money and what the bank paid for using it. Take the one piece of money from him. Give it to the one who has ten pieces of money." For the man who has will have more given to him. He will have more than enough. The man who has nothing, even what he has will be taken away. (Matthew 25:24–29, NIV)

Harsh reality that leads to another principle of money: it is our responsibility to do our part as co-laborers with Christ. Yes, we begin with prayer, and then we need to act. But how many of us are more like the last slave who buried the piece of silver in the ground? Certainly one perspective is that he was lazy and indifferent. But I think this poor fellow was simply afraid, and to that I can certainly relate. There have been times in my life when I not only buried my head in the sand but I feel like I flushed my money down the toilet. I was more incompetent than the last servant because I spent everything I made and more as soon as I got it. It took a long time for me to realize it was my responsibility not only to make money but to multiply it.

Our challenge is to leave fear behind and step out in wisdom. Empowered by God and His purpose for us, we can multiply our talents and He will guide us every step of the way if we just ask.

RESPONSIBILITY AT WORK

There seems to be an element conspicuously missing from the Proverbs 31 woman's story—her husband's role in her business plan. He's seen giving a positive reaction to her, he's known to sit among the elders of the land, but nowhere is he seen considering a field with his wife and making the real estate purchase or creating products and selling them for an income. It is this very capable lady who considers a field and buys it. *She* plants a vineyard. *She* does the work that we see accomplished here.

Though it's reasonable to assume that the husband wasn't excluded from all of her financial endeavors, I believe this passage is written this way so that all women ever since have a role model of someone who takes responsibility for herself and her family in every way, including financially. We don't see the woman of Proverbs 31 blaming her husband for being lazy or nagging him to get a better, higher-paying job. This was a woman of action. Instead of focusing on what her mate was or wasn't doing, she was focusing on her own work—at home, in the community, and in her business.

Let's be honest. What wife hasn't tried to change her spouse by some subtle suggestion for improvement or not-so-subtle criticism? The Proverbs 31 woman teaches us a better path—to love God, take care of our families and community, and take care of our finances, while enjoying the rewards of our hard work. She teaches us to take responsibility and to blame no one. And gentlemen, this goes both ways. Learning to be a good steward of money is part of God's spiritual plan for our lives.

QUESTIONS TO GO DEEPER

1. First let's begin with you. To successfully manage our families, our talents, and our finances, we must first accept and realize a crucial truth: we also have a responsibility to take care of ourselves. Why is it we still feel guilty about that? In embracing *The Proverbs 31 Financial Plan*, it's time for all of us to get over that guilt. "She girds herself with strength, and makes her arms strong" (verse 17). This lady stayed in shape, physically, mentally, and spiritually. She had to. And so do you. Are you

giving away too much of your time and energy and feeling resentful because of it? What can you do to strengthen your mind, body and spirit today?

_____

_____

_____

_____

_____

_____

2. Contemplate the sayings found in Proverbs 12:4, Proverbs 17:1, Proverbs 19:13–14, and Proverbs 21:9. How would you describe your current words, actions, and attitudes toward your husband or family in general? What impact might they be having on your loved ones?

_____

_____

_____

_____

_____

_____

3. What practical things can you do at home to become more like a woman who "looks well to the ways of her household" and receives the praise and blessings of her family? How can you bring more joy into the process?

_____

_____

_____

_____

_____

_____

_____

4. Who are you blaming for your financial problems? What is your responsibility for what you do and do not have?

_____

_____

_____

_____

_____

_____

_____

5. What principles can you learn from Proverbs 31:17 and Luke 5:15–16? "But the news about Him was spreading even farther, and large crowds were gathering to hear Him and to be healed of their sicknesses. But Jesus Himself would often slip away to the wilderness and pray." How will you apply these principles on taking responsibility to manage your time, your health, and your spiritual well-being?

_____

_____

_____

_____

_____

_____

6. Read the parable of the servants and talents. (Matthew 25:14–29)
    a. What are your thoughts on the third servant's actions?

_____

_____

_____

_____

_____

_____

b. What is your reaction to the master's response?

_____

_____

_____

_____

_____

_____

_____

c. How are you currently responding to the money, talents, and responsibilities God has given you? In what ways, if any, do you sense the Lord may want you to change?

_____

_____

_____

_____

_____

_____

_____

7. Brainstorm for a minute. What can you do today to make a positive difference in your family's financial future?

_____

_____

_____

_____

_____

_____

Whatever you do, do your work heartily, as for the Lord rather than for men, knowing that from the Lord you will receive the reward of the inheritance. It is the Lord Christ whom you serve.

(COLOSSIANS 3:23–24)

Notes:

_____

_____

_____

_____

_____

_____

_____

_____

_____

_____

_____

_____

_____

_____

_____

_____

CHAPTER 4

Love What Money Can Do, Not Money Itself

MONEY IS IMPORTANT, BUT THE Bible is clear that it cannot take first place in your life. If we're honest, that can be a real problem. Don't we spend a majority of our time in money-making activities? Don't we spend a good deal of effort thinking about how to advance our careers or bring more money into our homes? Don't we spend seventeen years or more in educational institutions, preparing for the work world so we can make good money?

And yet the Bible is straightforward, continuing in the book of Matthew:

> Do not store up for yourselves treasures on earth, where moth and rust destroy, and where thieves break in and steal. But store up for yourselves treasures in heaven, where neither moth nor rust destroys, and where thieves do not break in or steal…No one can serve two masters; for either he will hate the one and love the other, or he will be devoted to one and despise the other. You cannot serve God and wealth. (Matthew 6:19–20, 24)

Tough words. And these are words I have struggled with because I wondered how I could be free to serve God if I constantly had to work for money. Money was taking priority over my time and my thoughts. And yet God wanted me to multiply it, not just ignore it or reject it. But Jesus reminds us to keep it in perspective. Money cannot be first on your priority list. That's *God's* position. "Seek first His kingdom and His righteousness…" (Matthew 6:33) God is first. There *are* ways to fulfill our responsibility to multiply our money and be financially free without letting money be the "treasure" that we place at the top of our priority list.

PUTTING MONEY IN ITS PLACE

You've probably heard the verse "Money is the root of all evil," but that's a misquote of the Bible. Money isn't the problem; *loving* money is: "For the love of money is a root of all sorts of evil…" (1 Timothy 6:10) When you love money just for money's sake, you're in big trouble. It's a never-ending obsession that can never be quenched.

He who loves money will not be satisfied with money, nor he who loves abundance with its income. (Ecclesiastes 5:10)

Jesus also said, "It is easier for a camel to go through the eye of a needle than for a rich person to enter the kingdom." (Matthew 19:24, NCV) Again that doesn't mean God wants you to be poor. In fact, he promises spiritual riches for those who love and obey Him. But that statement from the Lord does indicate that money must not be a goal in and of itself.

As a coach with the Halftime Institute, I work with clients who sense God's purpose and calling in their lives but aren't sure how to get there. It's a feeling of holy discontent that the way we've lived in our first half of life may need to change to embrace significance in the second half of our lives. At some point we all question what exactly it is we're doing here. If we take that question to God, He'll give us the answer, but it may take some time and perseverance.

For me the change happened when I stopped asking the question "What's my plan for my life?" Instead I began asking God, "What is *your* plan for my life?" Like it or not, our resources either empower or hinder our purpose. Money is a part of our life's equation, but multiplying our money doesn't mean we're supposed to be obsessed with money. Money in its proper place is empowering. You can take it or leave it, and all is still well with your soul.

A century ago John D. Rockefeller was one of the wealthiest men on earth, but he reportedly said this: "I've made millions, but they brought me no real happiness. I'd barter them all for the days I sat on an office stool in Cleveland and counted myself rich on three dollars a week." Money itself will never bring us happiness. The truth is that most of us struggle to keep our finances in perspective. Year after year surveys indicate that money is the leading cause of conflict for America's couples. It's the stuff we fight about—because we give it the wrong priority.

Our Proverbs 31 woman put money in its place: It was a priority, but not first priority. She prospered financially but didn't let it affect her heart or change her desperation for God. She put the Lord before everything. She respected him and took action to care for her family in every way, including contributing financially. This right perspective allowed her to "sense that her gain was good" and to "smile at the future" without forgetting that her true spiritual riches were in God.

Remember again these words from Jesus:

I tell you, use the riches of this world to help others. In that way, you will make friends for yourselves. Then when your riches are gone, you will be welcomed into your eternal home in heaven. (Luke 16:9, NIRV)

QUESTIONS TO GO DEEPER

1. Now it's time to dream. At the Halftime Institute, we often ask questions similar to this: "If time, resources, or commitments were not a concern, describe three things you would still long to do?"

_____

_____

_____

_____

_____

_____

_____

2. If the above question stumps you, what are the first words that come to mind? It may help to draw your dream.

_____

_____

_____

_____

_____

_____

_____

3. Look forward ten years. You are attending a function where someone is giving a speech about you. Many of your closest friends and relatives are in attendance. What would you hope they would say about your impact on their lives?

_____

_____

_____

_____

_____

_____

_____

4. "The blessing of the Lord brings wealth, and he adds no trouble to it." (Proverbs 10:22) What is one regret you never want to have?

_____

_____

_____

_____

_____

_____

_____

5. As a means to an end, how have you seen the gift of money change your family or community for the better?

_____

_____

_____

_____

_____

6. God's dreams for you are always greater than anything you can imagine on your own. What would you like to accomplish to change someone's life?

_____

_____

_____

_____

_____

For we are His workmanship, created in Christ Jesus for good works, which God prepared beforehand so that we would walk in them. (Ephesians 2:10)

NOTES:

CHAPTER 5

Gratitude and Giving as a Game Changer

§

IN *WOMEN, TAKE CHARGE OF Your Money*, I wrote about one Easter morning in church, as the elders were passing around the offering plate. A woman sitting beside me only pretended to put money in the plate. She faked it—just went through the motions! At first I thought no one else saw it except me, but then I realized God had seen it too. God watches all of it, and shouldn't He be the only one who matters?

> And He sat down opposite the treasury, and began observing how the people were putting money into the treasury; and many rich people were putting in large sums. A poor widow came and put in two small copper coins, which amount to a cent. Calling His disciples to Him, He said to them, "Truly I say to you, this poor widow put in more than all the contributors to the treasury; for they all put in out of their surplus, but she, out of her poverty, put in all she owned, all she had to live on." (Mark 12:41–44)

I would have been tempted to feel superior to my miserly church neighbor had I not for years also cheated God. Like the multitude, I would contribute only from my surplus. Even when I finally got on board with giving to God financially—also known as tithing—it was far less than the 10 percent God suggested in the book of Malachi:

> "From the days of your fathers you have turned aside from My Laws and have not obeyed them. Return to Me, and I will return to you," says the Lord of All. "But you say, 'How are we to return?' Will a man rob God? Yet you are robbing Me! But you say, 'How have we robbed You?' You have not given Me the tenth part of what you receive and your gifts." (Malachi 3:7–8, NLV)

At tax time, in reviewing my charitable giving, I would think, "That's it? I could have sworn I gave more than that!" Not until I started taking this much more seriously did I finally experience the joy and true wealth that God offers to everyone who will step up to this plate when it comes to giving. You may have heard the following story before, but I'll tell it again: Just like everyone I know who has made this decision—yes, *everyone*—God blessed me remarkably. I actually had money left over after giving to God's work and paying my bills. I kept checking the account again and again to make sure I hadn't missed anything. I was giving more than I ever had, but I had more money left over.

How was it possible?

A DEAL WITH GOD

For almost four years, I worked with and learned from entrepreneur John Hewitt, who created both Jackson Hewitt and Liberty Tax Service. What many people don't realize about this very successful businessman is that he's also the cofounder of Stop Hunger Now and other world hunger organizations. As a deal maker, he says giving back to others became the game changer in his life:

I was struggling financially, I still wanted to tithe (donating traditionally 10 percent of income) but I couldn't mentally grasp it. I felt that I just didn't have enough money. So I made a deal with God. I said, "I can't afford to give 10 percent, but as soon as I get over this hump, I'm going to give way more than 10 percent." As soon as I started giving a lot of money, I received more and more. It seemed like that was an escalation point in my life and my business career. Giving became a game changer for me. This is where I formulated one of my theories: you can't give more than you receive. Some form of this principle is taught in many religious cultures, but here's the twist: when I give someone something, I'm not saying that person gives me something back—that almost never happens. Way more than 90 percent of the time they don't even appreciate it. Instead, overall, gifts in life come in from all different ways. It's not just financial gifts, it's emotional, health, everything. [2]

The lesson is we can't outgive God. His gifts may not be returned in the way you hope and the people to whom you give gifts may not even say thank you, but giving to God is our way to say thank you to Him.

Remember the Proverbs 31 woman. "She extends her hands to the poor; and she stretches out her hand to the needy." Not only was the Proverbs 31 woman providing for her family but she was contributing to her community. If you hope to be blessed in this world, you first have to bless others. Jesus taught this principle:

Then the King will say to those on his right, "Come, you who are blessed by my Father; take your inheritance, the kingdom prepared for you since the creation of the world. For I was hungry and you gave me something to eat, I was thirsty and you gave me something to drink,

---

2 John T. Hewitt, *iCompete: How My Extraordinary Strategy for Winning Can Be Yours* (Dallas: A Savio Republic Book, 2016), 197–98.

I was a stranger and you invited me in, I needed clothes and you clothed me, I was sick and you looked after me, I was in prison and you came to visit me."

Then the righteous will answer him, "Lord, when did we see you hungry and feed you, or thirsty and give you something to drink? When did we see you a stranger and invite you in, or needing clothes and clothe you? When did we see you sick or in prison and go to visit you?"

The King will reply, "I tell you the truth, whatever you did for one of the least of these brothers of mine, you did for me."

Then he will say to those on his left, "Depart from me, you who are cursed, into the eternal fire prepared for the devil and his angels. For I was hungry and you gave me nothing to eat, I was thirsty and you gave me nothing to drink, I was a stranger and you did not invite me in, I needed clothes and you did not clothe me, I was sick and in prison and you did not look after me."

They also will answer, "Lord, when did we see you hungry or thirsty or a stranger or needing clothes or sick or in prison, and did not help you?"

He will reply, "I tell you the truth, whatever you did not do for one of the least of these, you did not do for me." (Matthew 25:34–46, NIV)

When you give to anyone, it's as if you're giving to Jesus, Himself. That's the heart of giving financially to God. You may be able to fool everyone, but not Him. When the Israelites wanted to know how they were dishonoring God, He told them (through Malachi) that they were cheating Him out of their finances—"by taking your prize animals to market for top dollar, but bringing blind, lame and half-dead ones to my altar" (Malachi 1:7–8, TLB). Robbing God with your money deeply offends God and it also robs you of the blessings He wants to bring into your life.

God wants our best and He wants the best for us. Try it. He hopes you will trust Him with your money and honor Him with your wealth. I know this is challenging, but this is one area where He actually tells us to test Him. Listen to His words:

"Bring the tenth part into the store-house, so that there may be food in My house. Test Me in this," says the Lord of All. "See if I will not then open the windows of heaven and pour out good things for you until there is no more need." (Malachi 3:10, NLV)

Test Him in this. Give to the Lord, and see if He doesn't give back abundantly, beyond anything you might have expected or dreamed of for yourself. Then keep giving, even when you're tested (and you will be—but you'll also be victorious if you don't give up on giving). If you place your trust in the Lord and hold fast to the promises in His Word, you'll succeed in His way. Don't forget the Lord, and you'll prosper and be blessed in the work He has for you. And don't forget Him as you continue to experience success:

When you have eaten and are satisfied, praise the Lord your God. Praise him for the good land he has given you. Make sure you don't forget the Lord your God… But remember the Lord your God. He gives you the ability to produce wealth. That shows He stands by the terms of His covenant. He promised it with an oath to your people long ago. And He's still faithful to his covenant today. Don't forget the Lord your God… if you do, you will certainly be destroyed. (Deuteronomy. 8:10–11, 18–19, NIRV)

QUESTIONS TO GO DEEPER

1. Nowhere does the Lord promise that we'll all be millionaires; we will succeed only according to His will for our lives. When and how have you seen God miraculously provide for you and your family?

_____

_____

_____

_____

_____

2. What frightens you about giving? What do you have to lose by trying out the principle in Malachi 3:10 for at least one month?

_____

_____

_____

_____

_____

3. Reflect on this story and write three things you are thankful for today:

> While He was on the way to Jerusalem, He was passing between Samaria and Galilee. As He entered a village, ten leprous men who stood at a distance met Him; and they raised their voices, saying, "Jesus, Master, have mercy on us!"
>
> When He saw them, He said to them, "Go and show yourselves to the priests." And as they were going, they were cleansed.
>
> Now one of them, when he saw that he had been healed, turned back, glorifying God with a loud voice, and he fell on his face at His feet, giving thanks to Him. And he was a Samaritan.
>
> Then Jesus answered and said, "Were there not ten cleansed? But the nine—where are they? Was no one found who returned to give glory to God, except this foreigner?" (Luke 17:11–18)

_____

_____

_____

_____

_____

4. How can you express your gratitude to the Lord for everything he's given to you and your family?

_____

_____

_____

_____

_____

5. Don't you just hate it when you take time to do something nice for someone, and they don't even say thanks? If we're hurt by this, can you imagine how God feels as He reaches out His hands to us every day and we forget to thank Him? Here's a challenge: remember a time you have given to someone and received gifts or joy back from someone else?

_____

_____

_____

_____

_____

6. With thanksgiving, bring your requests before God to experience His peace. God loves a grateful heart. For everything created by God is good, and nothing is to be rejected if it is received with gratitude. (1 Timothy 4:4)

7. Write your requests on a prayer list, and monitor results as you keep praying. You'll be amazed how God shows up in surprising ways.

_____

_____

_____

_____

_____

8. Learn to be that one person in ten who thinks enough of God to look to Him and say, "Thank You!" Many of us turn to God in hard times; but learn to be one of those few who also turn to Him in prosperity and success. What one step will you take today?

_____

_____

_____

_____

_____

_____

Honor the Lord from your wealth, and from the first of all your produce; so your
barns will be filled with plenty, and your vats will overflow with new wine.

(Proverbs 3:9)

NOTES:

_____

_____

_____

_____

_____

_____

_____

_____

_____

_____

_____

_____

_____

_____

_____

_____

PART II

The Least You Need to Know About Money

CHAPTER 6

The Power of No and Yes

§

But remember the Lord *your God, for it is he who gives you the ability to produce wealth,
and so confirms his covenant, which he swore to your forefathers, as it is today.*

(Deuteronomy 8:18, NIV)

As we learned in Part I of *Divine Treasure*, once you've laid financial fear at the foot of the cross, there is one person who can make the biggest difference in your financial future: *you*. Entrepreneur John Hewitt has helped develop more than eight hundred millionaires in the tax companies he's founded over forty-eight years in his industry. One day in a corporate meeting, an employee asked a question we've probably all thought about at one time. "How do you become a millionaire?" John replied that most people would love to reach this goal, but the vast majority will not get there. In his distinctive, direct approach he told our team that the number-one reason you will or will not reach this goal is *you*. "Every day, you hold yourself back or propel yourself forward. A small percentage of the population becomes rich and it's not a magic formula. Hundreds of books have been written about it: *find something you like to do, work hard, and persevere.*"[3] Let me clarify an important point. *Divine Treasure* is not about how to become a millionaire. It is about a different type of abundance: becoming the best version—God's version—of yourself whether that means wealth or scarcity. I am not a proponent of the "prosperity gospel," teaching that God wants everyone to be rich. There was a point in the life of Jesus where He had no place to lay His head. (Matthew 8:20) The apostle Paul learned to be content in whatever circumstances he was in. "I know how to get along with humble means, and I also know how to live in prosperity; in any and every circumstance I have learned the secret of being filled and going hungry, both of having abundance and suffering need. I can do all things through Him who strengthens me." (Philippians 4:11–14, NASB)

On the other hand, there is nothing wrong with producing wealth, as long as it doesn't become your idol. You can pray (and God is very willing to work powerfully in your financial life) but even He

---

3 Ibid., 116.

requires you to take initiative before He does His greatest work, because "it is he who gives you the ability to produce wealth." (Deuteronomy 8:18)

Others can provide all kinds of great advice and opportunities to invest or run a business, but if you don't take action, nothing happens. If all you do is read, nothing will change for you. So are you tired of feeling like money just disappears from your wallet? If so—and if you're ready to *do something* about it—the next part of *The Proverbs 31 Financial Plan* contains the absolute bare minimum you need to know about money. The irony is this doesn't start with money; it starts with character and boundaries, knowing who you are and *who you are not*.

The Power of No

Do you believe being a "good Christian" means you should always say yes when requests are made? Not only is that not biblical, it's also not economical. If you always say yes to everyone who asks, you'll end up resenting them and disliking yourself. A mentor once told me that the way to distract someone from reaching their goals is to give them another goal. If you don't have a plan for your life, you can be sure that someone else will come up with a plan for you.

When I interviewed Dr. Henry Cloud, coauthor of the book *Boundaries*, he reminded me that being a good steward of your life is in no way being selfish, because our lives are a gift from God. Just as a store manager takes good care of a shop for the owner, we're to do the same with our souls—and I might add with our money. Our growth is God's "interest" on his investment in us. When we say no to people and things that hurt us or stretch us too thinly, we're protecting God's investment in us.

Let's try it:

"Can you work overtime tonight; we really need you to be a team player?"

All together now: "No!"

"Can you chair the school fund-raising committee this year, because you know, the children are relying on you?"

One more time: "No!" No plus no excuse.

So you think you're not quite ready for such an emphatic no? How about *wait*? Or, "Can I have some time to think about that?" Next time you're faced with a decision—any decision—resist the temptation to give an immediate response.

Remember the instruction that James, the brother of Jesus, gave us: "If any of you lacks wisdom, let him ask of God, who gives to all generously and without reproach, and it will be given to him." (James 1:5)

If you don't know what to do, or you feel guilty about saying no right away, then ask God, be patient, and you'll get your answer. This principle is so critical in the world of investing because we must learn to say no simply to protect ourselves. We must learn to be patient. We must also face the reality that not everyone is going to like us. Will everyone applaud you as you take your time making decisions? Definitely not. Will your financial advisor or real estate agent love you if you flat-out say no to their advice just because it doesn't sit well with you? You know the answer.

You may feel a little pull at your heart as you think about disappointing people, but now is the time to get over it. Learn to love saying no when the time calls for it.

Remember again how our Proverbs 31 woman considered a field before she bought it. She didn't just buy it right after she saw it. I imagine she said no to a couple of fields before she found her field of dreams. Think how contrary the principle of wise consideration is in our fast-paced world today. Haven't we all been tempted to dial the number on the TV screen for the latest money-making plan (with a ninety-day money-back guarantee)?

The Bible says we shouldn't be conformed to the ways and temptations of this world, but instead we should let God transform us through His teachings. I was asked to join a group of real estate investors who stressed the importance of making fast decisions. Many market investors echo this buy-now-think-later approach. But I don't. And never have. I can't tell you how many people have been aggravated at me because I say no to an investment that simply doesn't feel right. And if I feel I'm being pushed to make a fast decision before I'm completely comfortable with it, my answer is automatic: *No.*

If saying no is tough for me, waiting is harder. In making difficult decisions, I've found that the problem usually lies with my failure to listen, as opposed to the Lord not answering. When I jump into a decision without taking time to really hear the Lord, that's when I invariably make mistakes.

The Twenty-Four Hour Rule

I've found a simple strategy that works in helping me simply wait and listen. If I'm unsure of something or of which direction to take, I make it a rule to wait at least twenty-four hours before making my final decision. I might miss the deal of the decade, but I've found that a better deal will usually come along shortly. Waiting at least twenty-four hours gives me time to clear my head, get away from the emotions of the situation, and—most importantly—listen to the Lord.

If I'm facing a decision, I usually ask the Lord for wisdom before I go to bed at night. By morning I have the answer. God has given me the wisdom I need. Perhaps it was there all the time, but I just didn't perceive it. Sleep studies show that our brains are uniquely wired to process information, filtering what is most and least important, in these critical sleeping hours. Plus the quiet of the morning helps us to hear the Lord.

Removing myself from the intensity of the decision allows me to gain a completely different perspective. As I follow this approach, I'll sometimes even be aware of problems I didn't consciously notice at first. On some level, a spiritual level, I picked up what was wrong, but I couldn't put my finger on it until I asked for wisdom, waited, and listened.

Wait for God's still, calm voice and your quieted, untroubled mind to hear it.

THE POWER OF YES

Now that you've defined what you will *not* do, it's time to put on paper what you *will* accomplish. Let's call this "the power of yes." Some people call this goal setting, a concept which used to stress me out. I felt that once I put my goals on paper, I had to accomplish them or I would be a failure. I'm much kinder to myself now and much more fluid and flexible in handling my goals—the things in life I've chosen to say yes to. Truly many of the goals I had as a younger woman were flat-out wrong, not at all what God intended for my life. And many of the plans He had for me were far better than anything I might have dreamed up.

So why write your goals at all? Because when they're realistic and flexible, they become an important part of planning for your future. Remember, if you aim at nothing, you'll surely hit it. Another mistake I made in writing goals was expressing what I wanted out of life without stating how to get there. The how-tos are what get you somewhere—a good plan will slowly, eventually allow you to achieve the desires of your heart over time.

The Proverbs 31 woman had to spend time considering before she could act. She considered a field before she bought it. She looked for wool and flax to work with her hands. She planned for her children's futures and did not have fear about it, for all her household members were clothed with scarlet, the best material she could buy.

QUESTIONS TO GO DEEPER

Finding your path to yes takes time and asking yourself a few questions to begin.

1) "Delight yourself in the LORD; And He will give you the desires of your heart." (Psalm 37:4) What brings you the most joy and peace in your life?

_____

_____

_____

_____

_____

_____

_____

2) In the book *Too Busy Not to Pray*, Bill Hybels asks the question, "If you could ask God for one miracle in your life, knowing with 100 percent certainty that he would grant your request, what would you ask for?"

_____

_____

_____

_____

_____

_____

3) What has produced your best results in the past?

_____

_____

_____

_____

_____

4) If you had to take a guess right now, what do you absolutely feel you were put on this earth to do?

_____

_____

_____

_____

_____

5) What is holding you back or slowing you down?

_____

_____

_____

_____

_____

_____

6) When the task before you looks overwhelming, ask the Lord this one question: What is the next right step? What is one step I can take today to bring myself closer to the desires of your heart?

_____

_____

_____

_____

_____

_____

For You formed my inward parts; You wove me in my mother's womb.
I will give thanks to You, for I am fearfully and wonderfully made;
Wonderful are Your works, And my soul knows it very well.

(PSALM 139:13–14)

NOTES:

_____

_____

_____

_____

_____

_____

_____

_____

_____

_____

_____

_____

_____

_____

_____

_____

CHAPTER 7

Know Where You Stand Today

§

WITH MONEY IT'S EASY TO feel like you're climbing a slippery slope and your paychecks just don't seem to be making much progress up the hill. You might even be slipping backward, sucked down by rising expenses. I have good news for you. This is the part where we get down and dirty about the reality of our own financial situations. Even more than money, *The Proverbs 31 Financial Plan* is a tool to help drive your life's purpose. It's time to lift your head from the sand. These are just numbers—your personal numbers—and God is bigger than all of them. Wherever you are in life now can change for the better along with your financial picture, but the first thing you need to do is face today's reality. Knowing where you stand today means figuring out your current financial status.

Net worth is simply *what you own* minus *what you owe*. Let's say you own assets like houses, cars, or other valuables with a combined total value of $200,000. However, you owe the bank $100,000 for your house, you borrowed $10,000 for your children's education, and you've racked up $15,000 in credit card bills. Your net worth is $75,000 ($200,000 − $125,000 = $75,000).

Very simply, you increase your net worth by building your assets (for example, through investments) and getting rid of your debts. As you make these types of adjustments, your financial picture will change over time. It's important to calculate your net worth on a regular basis, at least once a year, so you can see whether or not it's improving. Knowing your net worth will also help you make decisions with your money so you can get closer to your goals.

So what *is* your net worth today—at this very moment? Let's find out.

WHAT YOU OWN

Start by making a list of everything you own and establishing an honest value for each item. In other words, if you own a home, don't use the price at which you'd like to sell it; use the actual amount for which you could sell it today, without making any improvements. Go through the same exercise with your other assets—personal property, automobiles, stocks, bonds, mutual funds, IRA accounts, CDs, savings accounts, whole life insurance policies with cash value, trust funds, rental property, and anything else that has value.

Use the following worksheet to document the value of all your assets, or make your own list using the worksheet as a guide. You may also want to enter these figures into an electronic spreadsheet. One benefit of doing this on a computer is that you can change the numbers in the future and easily calculate the new totals without having to do the arithmetic by hand. You can calculate net worth for you as an individual, or you can combine assets to calculate net worth for a couple. However, if you have separate property and expenses, you may want to do this separately for each individual wage earner in your family.

Worksheet A: Calculating Your Net Worth

SECTION A-1: ASSETS

Market Value of Owned Real Estate:
Primary Residence $_____
Secondary Residence (Rental Properties, Second Homes) $_____
Land and Commercial Property $_____
Personal Property:
Automobiles $_____
Jewelry $_____
Household Items (such as furniture, art, antiques) $_____
Other (such as collections, heirlooms) $_____
Other:
Cash (loose cash, checking account balance, piggy bank cash) $_____
Savings Account Balance(s) (include CDs, money market accounts) $_____
Stocks and Bonds (present market value) $_____
Life Insurance (cash value) $_____
IRA accounts $_____
401(k) and other Retirement/Pension Funds $_____
Trusts $_____
Other $_____
Total Personal Assets: $_____

What You Owe

So far, so good, right? Unfortunately, it's not the whole picture. Your assets count toward what's called your "gross net worth"—that is, what you're worth before subtracting out what you owe. Now it's time to see what parts of your assets actually belong to someone else. Let's look at your debts.

Use Section A-2 of Worksheet A to establish what you owe. Include mortgages, car loans, school loans, financing for your furniture, credit card balances, installment loans, and every type of debt that will have to be repaid. Use the total owed rather than the monthly payments; monthly payments matter for your budget, but total debt is what's important in figuring your net worth.

Also, order a copy of your credit report. You're entitled to one free report every year (visit www.annualcreditreport.com). This shows what the financial world believes you owe. Go through everything to make sure the information is accurate. If you find errors, contact the credit bureaus directly to dispute the amount (www.equifax.com, www.experian.com, www.tuc.com) so the errors can be corrected. In a subsequent *Divine Treasure* lesson, we'll take a deeper look at tackling debt and overcoming financial challenges. Remember, these are just numbers. They can and will change.

SECTION A-2: DEBTS

Real Estate Mortgages and Equity Loans on Real Estate Property:

Primary Residence $_____

Secondary Residence $_____

Land and Commercial $_____

Personal Property Debt:

Automobiles $_____

Financing on Household Items (such as furniture, electronics) $_____

Other Personal Property Debt $_____

Other:

School Loans $_____

Business Loans $_____

Credit Card Debt $_____

Personal Debt to Friends/Relatives $_____

Past Due Bills (such as medical, utilities) $_____

Other Loans or Debt $_____

Total Personal Debt: $_____

YOUR NET WORTH

Now, subtract your debts from your assets.

SECTION A-3: NET WORTH

Total Assets – Total Debt = Net Worth: $_____

You've just taken the first step toward facing your financial fears by facing reality. If you look at the numbers and find them depressing, don't crumple up the paper and chuck the entire process. You have to consider your situation as an opportunity rather than a problem. Now that you've done this work, it can help you make meaningful life changes to improve your situation. For instance, you may need to develop a plan to reduce your debt, or you might need to acquire more assets by purchasing a home, making investments, or committing to save more of your income each month.

On the other hand, if the numbers look better than you anticipated, don't think of it as a free pass to spend without limits. Instead, realize that you've just taken your first step toward greater financial stewardship. You're doing something positive for your future!

QUESTIONS TO GO DEEPER

1. What can you change today to make a difference this month?

_____

_____

_____

_____

_____

_____

_____

_____

2. What has worked for you already? How could you do more of that?

_____

_____

_____

_____

_____

_____

_____

3. What resources can help you?

_____

_____

_____

_____

_____

_____

_____

_____

4. Begin compiling a list of trusted advisors and mentors who can walk this path with you. We will devote a future lesson of *Divine Treasure* to building your team. For now remember the people in your life who love you unconditionally; the ones who really know you and have always "had your back."

_____

_____

_____

_____

_____

5. On a scale of one to ten, how motivated are you to making changes to your financial picture? What would it take to make it a ten?

_____

_____

_____

_____

_____

Come to me, all you who are weary and burdened, and I will give you rest.

(MATTHEW 11:28)

NOTES:

_____

_____

_____

_____

_____

_____

_____

_____

_____

_____

_____

_____

_____

_____

_____

_____

CHAPTER 8

Track What You're Making and Spending

§

Taking a hard look at your current numbers is just the beginning. The second step is tracking how you're using your money now to see where you can improve. It's like asking your doctor to diagnose you without ever being able to examine your symptoms. When you do some tracking and then look back at how much you make and where it goes each month, you can finally see if there are "viruses" in your spending habits. It's time for you to heal.

It might take some time to get everything organized, but you'll be glad when you realize the powerful impact tracking your income and expenses can have on your financial future. So pull out that bill file, dig around for those old income tax returns, and go through those drawers and closets where you've been stashing your financial history for years. Grab all the information you can find. It might take a day or two. Or you can work on this project one or two hours a day for several days. The important thing is doing it, not how long it takes.

As you work to identify all your income and expenses, create some order out of your information chaos by filing or storing your documents in a system that makes sense to you, electronically or the old fashioned way. When you're finished, you'll have the basis for your financial files in the future. You'll never have to start from scratch again.

When you have all of your past financial records available (tax returns, old bills, receipts, and credit card statements), use the following worksheet to record your average monthly totals for each income and expense category. You can do this in several ways. One approach is to make thirteen copies of Worksheet B and fill out one for each month (or use your own paper for monthly totals). Then calculate your monthly averages on the last copy.

The more realistic method for many people is to calculate income and expenses only twice, once for your most expensive month and once for your least expensive month. Maybe December, during the holiday frenzy, and February, when you're stuck at home trying to figure out how to recover from the holiday frenzy. Again, a computer spreadsheet like Worksheet B, will give you a firm foundation to work from in the future. Regardless of the method you choose, the important thing is that you'll end up with an honest and accurate dollar amount.

WORKSHEET B – TRACKING YOUR INCOME AND SPENDING

Month: _____ (Write the name of the month, or write "Yearly Average")

Section B-1 – My Income

Gross Amount of Salary, Wages, Tips, or Commissions (before taxes, insurance and other items are deducted)	$
Income from Rental Property	$
Dividends and/or Interest Income (from investments, savings accounts, CDs, money markets, etc.)	$
Money from Trusts, Pension Funds, Retirement Accounts, etc.	$
Payments received for Alimony or Child Support	$
Other Income	$
Total Gross Income (per month)	**$**

Section B-2 – My Taxes (Amounts withheld or paid out of salary, wages, & commissions)

Federal Taxes	$
State Taxes	$
Social Security Deductions	$
Local Taxes	$
Medicare deductions (if applicable)	$
Total Taxes I Owe (per month)	**$**

Section B-3 –My Spending

HOUSING-RELATED EXPENSES	
Mortgage Payment (include taxes and home insurance, if applicable)	$
Utilities	
Power (Electric, gas, fuel costs, etc.)	$
Water & Sewage	$
Waste Management	$
Rent Payment (if applicable)	$
Property Taxes (if not included in mortgage payment)	$
Condo or Homeowners Association Fees (if applicable)	$
Homeowners or Renters Insurance (if not included in mortgage payment)	$
Maintenance Expenses (home repair, improvements, etc.)	$
Phone service (in-home line)	$
Cell Phones	$
Internet Usage	$
Cable or Satellite Television	$
Home Services	
Lawn Care Service/Landscaping	$

Cleaning Service	$
Termite/Pest Control Service	$
TRANSPORTATION COSTS	
Car Payment	$
Automobile Insurance	$
Gas & Oil	$
Maintenance and Repair Expenses	$
Parking Fees	$
Road Tolls and Bridge Fees	$
Public Transportation Costs (Fares, Passes, etc.)	$
Insurance Premiums	
Health/Dental Insurance	$
Disability Insurance	$
Life Insurance	$
Other Insurance	$
Personal Care and Hygiene Spending	
Clothing	$
Hair Care	$
Laundry and/or Dry Cleaning (if not done at home)	$
Nail Care & Cosmetics	$
Other	$
Food Expenses	
Groceries (include all items regularly bought at the grocery store i.e. paper products, personal hygiene products, laundry & cleaning supplies)	$
Eating Out (include trips to restaurants, fast food, convenience stores)	$
Other	$
Medical Costs (include costs for children, if applicable)	
Insurance deductibles and other bills not covered by insurance	$
Doctor visit payments (if applicable)	$
Prescription drug costs	$
Medications bought over-the-counter	$
Other	$
Caring for My Children	
School Tuition Fees	$
Activity Expenses (Field Trips, Sports Teams, Music Lessons, etc.)	$
Clothing and/or Uniforms	$
Gifts	$
Child Support Payments and/or Child Care Costs	$
Other Expenses	$

ENTERTAINMENT AND EXTRAS	
Vacations	$
Health Club or Personal Fitness	$
Hobbies	$
Movies, Social Events, Dates, etc.	$
Books, Magazines, & Music	$
Clubs, Associations or other Group expense	$
Other	$
OTHER EXPENSES (Things that don't fall into other categories.)	
Debt Payments for Loans not already included above	$
Charitable Donations	$
A 'fudge factor' amount for things I might have forgotten	$

Section B-4 – Adding It All Up (per month)

My Current Spending Limit

INCOME LEFT OVER AFTER TAXES *(Total Gross Income minus Total Taxes I Owe)*	$

My Spending Habits

Total Housing Expenses	$
Total Transportation Expenses	$
Total Insurance Expenses	$
Total Personal Care and Hygiene Costs	$
Total Food Expenses	$
Total Medical Costs	$
Total Spending for My Children	$
Total Entertainment/Extra Spending	$
Total Misfit Expenses	$
TOTAL EXPENSES	$

Money I Can Save or Invest to Reach My Financial Goals:
(Subtract total expenses from income left over after taxes.)

$\$$_____

QUESTIONS TO GO DEEPER

1. At first glance, what surprises you most about this exercise?

_____

_____

_____

_____

_____

2. In what areas do you feel you can trim or cut altogether to give you more peace?

_____

_____

_____

_____

_____

3. Where do you feel you are doing best in your financial life? Give yourself credit for a job well done, and don't forget to thank God, who is the source of all of your provisions.

_____

_____

_____

_____

_____

_____

4. What are three actions you can take that would move you forward this week?

_____

_____

_____

_____

_____

_____

_____

5. How will you know when you have achieved your financial goals? What are the results you envision for your life?

_____

_____

_____

_____

_____

_____

Be anxious for nothing, but in everything by prayer and supplication with thanksgiving let your requests be made known to God. And the peace of God, which surpasses all comprehension, will guard your hearts and your minds in Christ Jesus.

(PHILIPPIANS 4:6–7)

NOTES:

CHAPTER 9

Determine Limits for Your Current Spending

❨

Yes, this chapter is about that dreaded work: budgeting. You may be cringing inside. Hardly anyone likes to talk about a budget, much less put one down on paper and live by it. And yet Calvin Coolidge once said, "There is no dignity quite so impressive, and no independence quite so important, as living within your means." [4]

Setting a budget helps you control your expenses and may even make you feel better about your financial condition. By experimenting with your budget figures on paper, you can make wiser decisions about whether or not you can afford a large purchase without creating a financial hardship. As you adjust your budget and learn to spend within your limits, you'll also free up money to save and invest, even if your income doesn't change. With more money saved, you're better prepared for life's financial surprises.

After examining your spending habits, you might discover your income doesn't support your expenses. Usually it's hard to make quick changes to your income. You can, however, have a quick and decisive impact on your spending. Lowering expenses can make a big difference at this stage of your money education. Overall, if you spend less, decrease your debt, and increase your savings and investments, you get to keep more of your money, which can be put to work for your future.

To establish your budget, use Worksheet C and record your average monthly expenses (from Worksheet B) for each category in the first column. Then go through your expenses and decide on realistic spending limits for each category. Put these new limits in the second column on Worksheet C.

Some of your expenses are fixed and can't be changed; for instance, your health insurance might have to stay the same (or even increase). But think carefully about where you *can* reduce your spending; those are the categories in which you can set lower limits. You might not need five cell phones in your family right now; perhaps you can reduce it to just two. Eat out just once a week as opposed to two or three times.

Your budget will be unique to *your* situation, but challenge yourself to reduce your spending. However, don't be so ambitious that you fill the final column with unrealistic numbers you'll never be able to meet.

---

4 http://www.notable-quotes.com/c/coolidge_calvin.html

When you're taking a good hard look at your spending, it's also important to consider the difference between needs, wants, and desires.

- *Needs* are basic requirements, such as food, clothing, shelter, and medical coverage.
- *Wants* involve choices about the quality of goods you buy. For instance, will you purchase new clothes or gently used clothes? Eat steak or hamburger? Buy a new car or a used car?
- *Desires* go above and beyond wants and can be purchased only out of what's left over when all other obligations have been met. Vacations, personal luxuries, and extra toys or gadgets would all be classified as desires.

When you think you've set reasonable limits for each spending category, add up your new budget figures (second column). Is this total less than your previous total monthly expenses (first column)? If so, you've reduced your spending and taken a huge step toward meeting your financial goals.

Now subtract your new total spending budget (second column) from the total monthly income (after taxes) that you calculated earlier on Worksheet B. The number you get represents the cash you'll have left over in your wallet or bank account each month if you follow your new budget. You can save or invest this extra cash to increase your net worth and your financial strength for the future. It can also serve as a cushion for emergencies.

Now that you've created a budget, stick to your plan by tracking your monthly expenses and keeping a close eye on how close you're coming to your budget limits. Guard carefully against complacency or lack of commitment. Creating a budget is the easy part; the challenge lies in sustaining the self-discipline to stick to it and not fall prey to your wants and desires. On the other hand, you also need to be flexible and realistic. In emergencies you may have to exceed your budget. And if your spending goes out of control, don't worry. Just recommit to your budget as soon as you can. Remember, these are just numbers.

If you're part of a family, following the budget will require the cooperation of every family member who spends household funds, so get everyone involved. You might even want to reward yourself or your family after a long period of success with your new budget. You can stash away some of your extra cash each month and use it for a family vacation, a special activity, or special gifts for one another.

WORKSHEET C – YOUR NEW BUDGET

Expense Category	Average Monthly Spending (Copy totals from Worksheet B)	Your New Spending Limit
HOUSING-RELATED EXPENSES		
Mortgage Payment	$	$
Utilities		
Power	$	$
Water & Sewage	$	$
Waste Management	$	$
Rent Payment	$	$
Property Taxes	$	$
Condo or Homeowners Association Fees	$	$
Homeowners or Renters Insurance	$	$
Maintenance Expenses	$	$
Phone service	$	$
Cell Phones	$	$
Internet Usage	$	$
Cable or Satellite Television	$	$
Home Services		
Lawn Care Service/Landscaping	$	$
Cleaning Service	$	$
Termite/Pest Control Service	$	$
TRANSPORTATION COSTS		
Car Payment	$	$
Automobile Insurance	$	$
Gas & Oil	$	$
Maintenance and Repair Expenses	$	$
Parking Fees	$	$
Road Tolls and Bridge Fees	$	$
Public Transportation Costs	$	$
INSURANCE PREMIUMS		
Health/Dental Insurance	$	$
Disability Insurance	$	$
Life Insurance	$	$
Other Insurance	$	$

PERSONAL CARE AND HYGIENE SPENDING		
Clothing	$	$
Hair Care	$	$
Laundry and/or Dry Cleaning	$	$
Nail Care & Cosmetics	$	$
Other	$	$
FOOD EXPENSES		
Groceries	$	$
Eating Out	$	$
Other	$	$
MEDICAL COSTS		
Insurance deductibles and other bills not covered by insurance	$	$
Doctor visit payments	$	$
Prescription drug costs	$	$
Medications bought over-the-counter	$	$
Other	$	$
CARING FOR MY CHILDREN		
School Tuition Fees	$	$
Activity Expenses	$	$
Clothing and/or Uniforms	$	$
Gifts	$	$
Child Support Payments and/or Child Care Costs	$	$
Other Expenses	$	$
ENTERTAINMENT AND "EXTRAS"		
Vacations	$	$
Health Club or Personal Fitness	$	$
Hobbies	$	$
Movies, Social Events, Dates, etc.	$	$
Books, Magazines, & Music	$	$
Clubs, Associations or other Group expense	$	$
Other	$	$
MISFIT EXPENSES		
Debt Payments for Loans not already included above	$	$
Charitable Donations	$	$
A 'fudge factor' amount for things I might have forgotten	$	$
TOTALS (Add all rows in both columns)	**$**	**$**

Debt is an important part of your financial equation. So important that we'll devote a separate lesson to becoming victorious in this area and tacking other challenges. For now the least you need to know is your debt-to-income ratio. To figure this out, use the table below to determine your total monthly outlay for debt payments.

Debt Category	Monthly Amount
Housing Debt (mortgage or rent)	$
Loan Payments	$
Equity Lines of Credit Payments	$
Revolving Credit Payments (financing on furniture or appliances)	$
Credit Card Payments (minimum monthly payment)	$
Alimony/Child Support	$
Other monthly debt payments	$
TOTAL MONTHLY DEBT LOAD	**$**

Now divide your total monthly debt load by your total monthly income (after taxes) that you calculated on Worksheet B. The resulting percent is your debt-to-income ratio. Lenders use this ratio to determine how much they can allow you to borrow, and you can use this ratio to examine whether you're too far in debt. The idea is that the higher your ratio, the harder it will be for you to make your payments out of your current income. While every situation is different, general rules about debt-to-income ratios include the following:

* 40 percent or more means your credit situation is out of control. You need to take immediate action, including seeking wise counsel from a nonprofit credit counseling organization. Make sure this is a free service and they aren't trying to sell you anything.
* 36 to 40 percent puts you in the borderline category. You may be approved for more credit, but paying the bills on time will be a struggle.
* 30 to 36 percent is OK. Lenders should have no problem loaning you money, but you're still not in the best possible position.
* Under 30 percent—You're doing well, but you need to watch your other expenses so you can maintain this low level of debt.

QUESTIONS TO GO DEEPER

1. After calculating your new budget limits, what items emerge as your basic *needs?* These are the absolute necessities and basic requirements of life.

_____

_____

_____

_____

_____

_____

_____

2. Remember, *wants* involve choices about the quality of goods you buy. These are over and above your basic needs in life. What adjustments can you make in this category for a positive future?

_____

_____

_____

_____

_____

_____

_____

3. *Desires* go above and beyond wants and needs. These are acquired with what's left over after you've met your other obligations. What do you most desire in your financial life?

_____

_____

_____

_____

_____

_____

_____

4. Taking desires to the next level, what is it you most desire that can't be purchased with money?

_____

_____

_____

_____

_____

_____

_____

5. Where do you feel you can adjust your priorities to create a balanced budget, giving you hope for your future?

_____

_____

_____

_____

_____

_____

"For I know the plans that I have for you," declares the Lord, *"plans for welfare and not for calamity to give you a future and a hope."*

(Jeremiah 29:11)

Notes:

CHAPTER 10
Smile at Your Future

§

WE STARTED THIS JOURNEY WITH the Proverbs 31 woman. Circling back to her, something has always stood out to me: she smiled at the future. She worked with her hands in delight. She sensed that her gain was good. With her security first in God, she was able to smile at the future for many reasons, one of which was the reality that she planned for the future. She wasn't afraid of winter, because she'd prepared her household for it. She'd made the best clothing she could find for herself and her family.

Strength and dignity were also her clothing. She was able to smile at the future because she'd invested in a business—a vineyard that would feed her children and her children's children long after she was gone. The Proverbs 31 woman also laughed at the days to come, because she wouldn't let doubt creep into her plans. She trusted in God, who's bigger than any challenge, obstacle, or hardship she would encounter. She smiled at the future because she was ready for it.

The Bible teaches us to "know where you are headed, and you will stay on solid ground." (Proverbs 4:26, CEV) If you were going to spend a year at sea on a boat, it would take planning, as would building a sports team or running for public office. Almost everything worthwhile requires some level of planning; achieving excellent financial stewardship is no different. You need specific goals and a plan for achieving them. If you aim at nothing, you'll likely to end up nowhere with nothing. Do you really want to allow chance or other people to dictate your financial future? Do you want to passively accept what the world throws at you and pretend you can't change a thing? You might find yourself up the proverbial creek without a proverbial paddle. Don't leave yourself vulnerable when it's in your power to make a difference.

Now even if you've got a steel trap for a mind, life makes it tough to remember, work toward, and achieve your goals if they're not written down. Financial goals written on paper are always more real than those that stay in your head. Written goals have a way of feeling "official" and undeniable. They're harder to rationalize away. And written goals are easier to modify and refer back to when things get tough. So get out your laptop, phone, or just another sheet of paper, and get ready to make some plans.

Different goals require different time periods. You might reach some goals in weeks or months, and others might take years. Some goals depend on achieving other goals first. For instance, a long-term retirement goal might depend upon a mid-term investment goal. For most of us, our goals fluctuate from time to time, as priorities and conditions change. For that reason, it's usually better to establish short-term, mid-term, and long-term objectives. And you need to remain flexible.

Long-Term Goals

Long-term objectives don't generally change as circumstances change, and they focus on our desire for financial peace, a comfortable retirement, or enough savings and passive income that money is no longer a concern. Or maybe you're planning for your children's education; it's not too early to do this when they're still infants. These goals for the distant future need to be realistic, but they can also be ambitious—particularly if you're setting them early in life. Bear in mind that meeting long-term financial objectives takes discipline. If you dip into long-term funds, you may miss your goals. Take your long-term objectives seriously.

Mid-Term Goals

Each person has to determine a time frame for mid-term objectives, but these are typically three to ten years in the future. This category might include saving for a down payment on a house or condo, for an advanced degree, for a child's private school tuition, for a family vacation, or for a new or used car.

Mid-term goals might also include investments with an eye toward a target net worth or a specific amount of money in mutual funds or IRAs. Paying off car loans, equity lines of credit, or other debt might be among your mid-term goals. Mid-term objectives often change as your situation does—think weddings, babies, and unexpected financial needs. Usually these goals require substantial amounts of money, but not so much that it's impossible to save what you need. *Saving* for mid-term goals is a wiser choice than paying for them on credit and increasing your debt load.

Short-Term Goals

Short-term objectives are usually "where the action is" (and where the pitfalls are). These are goals between one and three years out into the future, and they might include paying off credit card debt; retiring an automobile loan or being in a position to take one on, and taking on a home-improvement project.

Obviously your current financial situation—your assets and liabilities—will determine where specific financial objectives fall along your timeline. Here are several guidelines for establishing your goals:

- Write your goals down on paper (or on your computer) in a form that you can easily reference.
- Don't make your goals so far-fetched you can never hope to achieve them. For example, if you take home $2,000 a month after taxes, and you have regularly occurring expenses of $1,400, you can't realistically expect to be a millionaire in ten years without some major changes. If you don't choose attainable goals, you'll get so frustrated you might give up on the whole process.
- Try not to overwhelm yourself. As a rule, state no more than five objectives for each time frame (short-term, mid-term, and long-term).
- Review your financial objectives every three months, and see if they're still relevant.
- When circumstances change, make a trip to the financial file, and evaluate the impact on your goals. A pay raise might mean pushing a goal's time frame up since you can pay off more debt earlier or save more toward the future. On the flip side, major dental work might require moving a car purchase back a few months or a year.
- Don't completely throw away goals that change or just need adjustments. A turn of events may allow you to add an objective back into your plan in the future.
- Dream big and take small steps! While you want to stay realistic, you also need to give yourself the freedom to plan for a meaningful and significant future. Some or all of your dreams can and will come true.

YOUR PLAN OF ACTION

Some possibilities to consider for short-term goals:

- Reduce your debt by 20 percent.
- Increase your savings by 20 percent.
- Take the first steps to begin a college savings plan for your children.
- Pay off a high-interest credit card.

1. Write three to five short-term objectives that could change your life.

_____

_____

_____

_____

_____

_____

2. Some goals to consider for mid-term time frames:

- Save enough for a house down payment.
- Put enough money in an accessible account for a ninety-day emergency cushion—and never tap it for regular expenses.
- Save enough to pay for a wedding.
- What are three to five mid-term goals that would give more financial hope for you and your family?

_____

_____

_____

_____

_____

_____

3. Some possible long-term objectives:

- Pay off a house mortgage early.
- Become debt-free.
- Invest for adequate passive retirement income.

Imagine you are eighty years old, and you are looking back at your life. What have you achieved? Write three to five long-term goals that are most important to you.

_____

_____

_____

_____

_____

4. From the above list, what rewards would personally mean the most to you? What do you value most highly?

_____

_____

_____

_____

_____

_____

_____

5. How can you bring more celebration and joy into this process? Remember to choose some goals that are just for fun!

_____

_____

_____

_____

_____

_____

I now understand from my own experience coaching clients, as well as from reporting on hundreds of human-interest stories over the years, that our attitudes toward life will absolutely determine our outcomes. If you believe you'll never be able to handle your financial life, you'll be right. If you believe handling money successfully just isn't in your gene pool, you're right. You're limited only by your beliefs! Conversely, if you believe you can successfully get a grip on your finances, then you will. If you believe God requires us to be responsible with our money, then know also that He'll give you the resources and the wisdom to handle it.

If God expects us to multiply our money (talents), then He'll show you how in your own life. Plus, God's provision will allow you to have hope for the future and work with your hands in delight. The end result will be sensing that your gain is good. That's a promise—God's promise.

"Let those who favor my righteous cause and have pleasure in my uprightness shout for joy and be glad, and say continually, 'Let the Lord be magnified, who takes pleasure in the prosperity of His servant'" (Psalm 35:27).

God wants you to prosper and to be blessed in every area of your life so you can be a blessing to others. God has big plans for your life; His dreams for you are greater than anything you can imagine on your own. But believing God wants you well—in body, mind, soul, and pocketbook—takes a decision on your part. A choice to search for what is good. A decision to look for what is positive about you and your situation, according to the standards so graciously given to us in scripture:

Whatever is true, whatever is honorable, whatever is right, whatever is pure, whatever is lovely, whatever is of good repute, if there is any excellence and if anything worthy of praise, dwell on these things. (Philippians 4:8)

And smile at your future.

Notes:

SOURCES CONSULTED

Bundesen, Lynn. *The Woman's Guide to the Bible.* New York: Crossroad Publishing Company, 1993.

Burkett, Larry. *How to Manage Your Money.* Chicago: Moody Press, 1982.

Castleberry, Carolyn. *Women, Get Answers About Your Money: Because There Are No Dumb Questions About Personal Finance.* Oregon: Multnomah, 2006.

———. *Women, Take Charge of Your Money: A Biblical Path to Financial Security.* Oregon: Multnomah, 2006.

Cloud, Henry, and John Townsend. *Boundaries.* Grand Rapids, MI: Zondervan, 1992.

Devine, William Francis, Jr. *Women, Men and Money.* New York: Harmony Books, 1998.

Drake, Marsha. *The Proverbs 31 Lady and Other Impossible Dreams.* Minneapolis: Bethany House Publishers, 1984.

Faerber, Esme. *The Personal Financial Calculator.* New York: McGraw-Hill, 2003.

George, Elizabeth. *Beautiful in God's Eyes.* Eugene, OR: Harvest House Publishers, 1998.

Hayes, Christopher, and Kate Kelly. *Money Makeovers: How Women Can Control Their Financial Destiny.* New York: Doubleday, 1997.

Hewitt, John T. *iCompete: How My Extraordinary Strategy for Winning Can Be Yours.* Dallas, Texas: A Savio Republic Book 2016.

Kiyosaki, Robert, and Sharon Lechter. *Cashflow Quadrant: Rich Dad's Guide to Financial Freedom.* New York: Warner Business Books, 2000.

———. *Rich Dad, Poor Dad.* New York: Warner Business Books, 2000.

McLean, Andrew James, and Gary W. Eldred. *Investing in Real Estate.* 4th ed. Hoboken, NJ: John Wiley and Sons, 1988.

Reid, E. R. *The Proverbs 31 Woman: A Study Aid.* Shippensburg, PA: Destiny Image Publishers, 1993.

Rosenberg, Stephen M., and Ann Z. Peterson. *Every Woman's Guide to Financial Security.* Franklin Lakes, NJ: Career Press, 1997.

Sheets, Charleton. *How to Buy Your First Home or Investment Property with No Down Payment.* Burr Ridge, IL: Profession Education Institute, 1999.

Spangler, Ann, and Jean E. Syswerda. *Women of the Bible.* Grand Rapids, MI: Zondervan, 1999.

GIVING BACK

Carolyn Castleberry Hux is available for speaking events and for every copy of *Divine Treasure: The Proverbs 31 Financial Plan to Give You Hope for Your Future* purchased for your attendees, Carolyn will donate $1/book back to your non-profit. For more information, email faithandwomen@gmail.com

Carolyn is the Founder and President of Faith and Women Ministries, Inc., a 501(c)(3) non-profit, public charity. She has more than 30 years of experience in leadership development, trained as a servant leader with Campus Crusade for Christ and currently serving as a Master Certified Halftime Coach with the Halftime Institute. Carolyn works one-on-one with leaders to help them invest their second half of life where it matters most. Her book, *It's About Time: 10 Smart Strategies to Avoid Time Traps and Invest Yourself Where it Matters* provides strategies for maximum impact and significance.

Carolyn is a nationally recognized author with Simon and Schuster and Random House, and a former television news anchor in Virginia and Colorado, and co-host for Living the Life on ABC Family Channel. Carolyn's work has been featured on FOX and Friends, USAToday.com, MSN Money, Essence magazine, and major newspapers and radio programs in the U.S. and Canada. She hosted the first national radio talk show for female executives on the Business Radio Network, "Women Talk Business," which was recognized by the American Women in Radio and Television.

Carolyn worked as a financial advisor with Series 7 and 66 registrations. Her books include, *Women, Take Charge of Your Money: A Biblical Path to Financial Security* and *Women, Get Answers about Your Money: because there are no dumb questions about personal finance.*

Printed by Amazon Italia Logistica S.r.l.
Torrazza Piemonte (TO), Italy

37420846R00063